B2B

Business-to-Business Basic Guide
Geo Report
2023

Chapter 1: Introduction to B2B

1.1 What is B2B (Business-to-Business)?

Business-to-Business (B2B), or "Business to Business", is a commercial transaction model that involves the buying and selling of products, services or information between companies, as opposed to transactions aimed at the end consumer, known as Business-to-Consumer (B2C). In the context of B2B, a company acts as a customer of another company, whether to acquire products that will be used in its internal operations, resell to other customers or integrate into its own products and services.

B2B is a fundamental part of the global economy, underpinning a wide range of industries, from manufacturing and technology to financial services and logistics. In this model, companies often purchase in larger quantities and often in longer cycles than individual consumers. This is because companies often need consistent supplies to keep their operations running, which can involve complex sourcing, production and distribution processes.

This commercial relationship involves several aspects:

1. Specialized Products and Services: B2B covers products and services that meet the specific needs of companies. It can range

from raw materials for manufacturing to customized software to optimize internal processes.

2. Long-Term Relationships: Due to the nature of purchasing, B2B relationships tend to be longer-lasting and built on trust. Companies look for reliable and consistent suppliers.

3. Personalized Negotiations: B2B transactions often involve more complex negotiations, as each company's needs are unique. This may include prices, delivery times, product specifications, etc.

4. Consultative Sales: Sales in the B2B model are often consultative, involving a deep understanding of customer needs and offering personalized solutions.

5. Influence on the Supply Chain: The efficiency and quality of products and services provided by companies in the B2B model can impact the entire supply chain and, by extension, the quality of the final product or service provided by the purchasing company.

B2B is the backbone of many economic activities, contributing to manufacturing, distribution and service delivery across multiple industries. Companies operating in this model play interdependent roles, forming a complex network of collaboration and transactions that keeps the economy running efficiently.

1.2 Importance of B2B in the economy

Business-to-Business (B2B) plays a fundamental role in the global economy, being the backbone that supports the functioning of various industries and sectors. This type of commercial transaction not only enables the circulation of products and services between companies, but also significantly boosts economic growth. Here are some key points that highlight the importance of B2B in the economy:

1. Integrated Supply Chain: B2B is essential for creating and maintaining efficient supply chains. Companies that supply inputs, components and raw materials play a crucial role in ensuring that other companies can produce, assemble and deliver final products to consumers.

2. Fostering Innovation: Interdependence between companies in the B2B model encourages innovation. Companies collaborate to develop more advanced products and services, resulting in continuous improvements and technological advances that benefit the entire industry.

3. Job Creation: The demand generated by B2B transactions creates jobs at various stages of the production chain. From manufacturing to distribution and marketing, B2B generates employment opportunities across a wide range of sectors.

4. Stimulating Economic Growth: B2B boosts economic growth by stimulating business activity. As companies become successful, they expand their operations, hire more employees, and contribute to the increase in the country's Gross Domestic Product (GDP).

5. Regional Development: B2B often stimulates the development of specific regions. Concentrations of companies that provide inputs or specialized services can form, creating economic hubs and boosting local development.

6. International Trade: B2B is also the basis of international trade. Companies export and import products and services in B2B transactions, contributing to the globalization of the economy.

7. Economic Stability: Diversification of B2B transactions helps distribute risks. If one industry is affected by economic challenges, others can continue operating, avoiding significant imbalances in the economy.

8. Sustainability: Cooperation in the B2B model can lead to more sustainable practices. Companies that supply components or materials can work together to reduce waste and minimize environmental impact.

9. Investments and Financing: B2B transactions also have an impact on financial markets. Companies can seek investment and financing to expand their operations, boosting overall economic activity.

B2B is a crucial cog in the global economic machine. Interactions between companies, their collaboration and mutual dependence are fundamental factors for the growth, innovation and sustainability of economies around the world.

1.3 Differences between B2B and B2C (Business-to-Consumer)

The fundamental differences between B2B (Business-to-Business) and B2C (Business-to-Consumer) business models center on the types of transactions, target audience and marketing and sales strategies. Here are the main distinctions between these two models:

1. Target Audience and Customers:
- B2B: In the B2B model, transactions are directed to other companies. Buying companies are seeking products or services for use in their business operations. The focus is on meeting the specific needs of the business and the demands of the corporate market.
- B2C: In the B2C model, transactions are directed to individual consumers. Companies sell products or services directly to end consumers, seeking to satisfy the personal needs and preferences of individuals.
2. Purchase Volume:
- B2B: In B2B, purchase quantities tend to be larger, as companies often need consistent supplies for their operations.
- B2C: In B2C, purchase quantities are generally smaller, as they meet the individual needs of consumers.
3. Purchase Complexity:
- B2B: Purchasing decisions in B2B are often more complex, involving considerations such as return on investment, integration with existing systems and specific operational needs.
- B2C: Purchasing decisions in B2C can be influenced by emotional, aesthetic and convenience factors, making them sometimes less complex than in B2B.
4. Relationships and Interactions:
- B2B: B2B transactions generally involve long-term relationships, built on mutual trust and the consistent delivery of value over time.
- B2C: B2C transactions can be more transactional and short-term, with less emphasis on building lasting relationships.
5. Marketing and Sales Strategies:
- B2B: B2B marketing strategies emphasize education, providing detailed information about how products or services can solve specific business problems. Sales is often consultative, with a focus on presenting customized solutions.
- B2C: B2C marketing strategies often appeal to emotions, values and experiences. Sales can be boosted by creative and appealing marketing campaigns.
6. Sales Cycle:
- B2B: The sales cycle in B2B tends to be longer, due to the complexity of decisions and the need to establish trust.
- B2C: The sales cycle in B2C can be shorter, as individual consumers can make purchasing decisions more quickly.
7. Distribution Channels:

- B2B: Distribution channels in B2B can involve distributors, resellers and business partners to reach a wider business audience.

- B2C: Distribution channels in B2C often involve direct sales, physical and online retail.

The differences between B2B and B2C models impact every aspect of business, from target audience to marketing, sales and customer relationship strategies. Each model requires different approaches to meet the unique needs and expectations of their respective audiences.

1.4 Benefits and challenges of B2B

The Business-to-Business (B2B) model offers a series of benefits to companies, while at the same time presenting specific challenges. Here are the main benefits and challenges of B2B:

Benefits of B2B:

1. Volume Transactions: B2B transactions often involve buying and selling in volume, allowing companies to obtain supplies, raw materials or finished products in larger quantities, which can lead to economies of scale and reduced unit costs.

2. Long-Term Relationships: B2B generally promotes building long-term relationships between companies. Mutual trust and ongoing collaboration are valued, creating stable and mutually beneficial partnerships.

3. Personalization and Customization: In B2B, it is common for products and services to be customized to meet the specific needs of each customer. This can lead to more appropriate and relevant solutions for buying companies.

4. Greater Added Value: Products and services sold in B2B often add more value than those aimed at the end consumer. This is because purchasing companies often look for solutions that can improve their own operations.

5. Sustainable Growth: Long-term relationships and continuous demand for B2B products and services contribute to more sustainable growth over time.

B2B challenges:

1. Complex Negotiations: Negotiations in the B2B model tend to be more complex due to the nature of the transactions and the need to reach agreements that meet the expectations of both parties.

2. Prolonged Sales Cycles: Sales cycles in B2B are often longer due to detailed negotiations, more complex decision making and rigorous assessments of costs and benefits.
3. Dependence on Partners: In B2B, companies often depend on suppliers and partners to ensure that products and services are delivered with quality and on time. Any failure in the supply chain can affect operations.
4. Greater Financial Risks: Due to the volume and value of B2B transactions, the associated financial risks can be significant. Companies need to carefully weigh the risks and rewards before closing deals.
5. Group Decisions: In many cases, B2B purchasing decisions involve multiple stakeholders and decision makers within an organization. This can complicate the decision-making process and lengthen the sales cycle.

The B2B model offers advantages such as volume transactions and long-term relationships, but it also presents challenges such as complex negotiations and prolonged sales cycles. Companies operating in the B2B market need to manage these challenges while capitalizing on the unique benefits this model can provide.

1.5 Current trends in the B2B market

Certainly, the B2B market is undergoing significant transformations driven by technological advances and changing customer expectations. Here are some current trends that are shaping the B2B environment:
1. Digitalization of Buying and Selling Processes: As in the B2C market, digitalization is becoming a fundamental part of B2B. Online platforms and B2B marketplaces are emerging, making it easier for businesses to search, compare and purchase products and services from suppliers around the world.
2. Personalization of B2B Experiences: Just as consumers expect personalized experiences, B2B companies are also seeking personalization. This involves offering tailored recommendations, dynamic pricing based on customer needs, and providing more focused sales support.
3. Growing Importance of Digital Marketing: Digital marketing is gaining ground in the B2B environment. Companies are using

strategies like content marketing, SEO (search engine optimization), and social media to connect with potential buyers and build their online presence.

4. Data Analytics and Artificial Intelligence: B2B companies are leveraging data analytics and artificial intelligence to better understand customer behavior, predict demand trends, and enhance the personalization of their offerings.

5. Process Automation: Automation is improving efficiency in multiple areas of B2B, from supply chain to customer service. This not only reduces errors, but also frees up human resources for higher value-added tasks.

6. Marketplaces and Supplier Networks: Marketplace platforms are becoming more popular in B2B, allowing companies to buy and sell in a consolidated online environment. In addition, supplier networks are being formed to facilitate collaboration and information sharing.

7. Focus on Sustainability and Social Responsibility: Concern about sustainability is being reflected in B2B, with companies looking for partners that adopt ethical, environmentally conscious and socially responsible practices.

8. Augmented Reality (AR) and Virtual Reality (VR): AR and VR are being used to improve the B2B experience, allowing customers to view products more immersively and conduct virtual training, for example.

9. Purchasing Through Mobile Devices: Just like consumers, B2B buyers are using mobile devices to make purchases. This requires companies to optimize their platforms for mobile devices.

10. Global Expansion: Digitalization and connectivity are enabling B2B companies to expand their markets globally, reaching new customers in different parts of the world.

These trends are transforming the way B2B companies operate, interact with their customers and partners, and manage their operations. Adapting to these changes is essential to remain competitive in the ever-evolving B2B marketplace.

Chapter 2: B2B Marketing Strategies

2.1 B2B market segmentation

Market segmentation in the Business-to-Business (B2B) context is an essential strategy that aims to divide the market into specific groups of companies that share similar characteristics and needs. This approach helps companies understand their customers better, adapting their marketing and sales strategies more effectively. Here is a detailed explanation of B2B market segmentation:

What is B2B Market Segmentation?

B2B market segmentation involves careful analysis of buyer companies to identify different groups with similar characteristics. These characteristics can include company size, industry, geographic location, purchasing behavior, specific needs, and more. The idea is to create segments that are homogeneous internally and heterogeneous among themselves.

Benefits of Segmentation in B2B:

1. In-Depth Customer Knowledge: Segmentation allows companies to better understand who their customers are and what their specific needs are. This makes it possible to create more relevant and targeted offers.

2. Customization of Marketing Strategies: By dividing the market into segments, companies can create messages, content and offers that resonate better with each group. This leads to more personalized and effective marketing strategies.

3. Campaign Efficiency: By targeting marketing efforts to specific segments, companies can avoid wasting resources on audiences that are not relevant to their products or services.

4. Increased Conversion Rate: When communicating with companies that have similar needs, the probability of conversion increases, as the message is more in line with what the customer is looking for.

B2B Market Segmentation Process:

1. Data Collection: Companies collect relevant data about their client companies, such as size, industry, location, purchase history, etc.

2. Data Analysis: The collected data is analyzed to identify common patterns and characteristics among companies.

3. Definition of Segments: Based on the analysis, segments are defined. Each segment represents a homogeneous group of companies.

4. Segment Profile: Each segment is detailed with information about needs, preferences, purchasing behavior and specific characteristics.

5. Strategies Development: Based on segment profiles, companies develop customized marketing and sales strategies for each group.

Practical example:

Imagine a company that sells IT equipment. It can segment its market into segments such as small retail companies, mid-sized healthcare companies, and large financial corporations. Each segment will have different needs, such as security requirements, infrastructure size and budget. The company will be able to create specific messages for each segment and offer solutions that meet these individual needs.

B2B market segmentation is a vital component to successful marketing and sales strategies. It allows companies to approach their customers more precisely, providing solutions that perfectly align with their needs, resulting in stronger and more successful relationships.

2.2 Development of personas in the B2B context

Developing personas in the Business-to-Business (B2B) context is a valuable strategy that allows companies to better understand their target customers and target their marketing actions more effectively. Personas are fictional, detailed representations of target companies that help bring data to life and understand those companies' needs, challenges, goals, and behaviors. Here's a detailed look at the importance of personas in B2B marketing:

Importance of Personas in B2B Marketing:

1. Deep Understanding of Customers: B2B personas go beyond basic demographics. They dive into details about companies such as industry, size, organizational structure, business objectives and specific challenges.

2. Targeting Messages: By creating personas, companies can adapt their messages and content according to the specific needs of each

customer segment. This leads to more relevant and meaningful communications.

3. Customization of Marketing Strategies: Personas allow companies to develop personalized marketing strategies for each segment. This includes decisions about communication channels, tone of voice, visual style and overall approach.

4. Generation of Qualified Leads: With well-defined personas, companies can attract and nurture leads that fit the profile of their personas. This leads to more qualified and relevant lead generation for the business.

5. Development of Relevant Content: By understanding the concerns and challenges of target companies, personas guide the creation of content that directly addresses these issues. This helps build trust and establish the company as a trusted source of information.

6. Improved Customer Experience: Well-developed personas allow companies to design tailored experiences for their customers. This ranges from the first contact to post-sales, increasing customer satisfaction and loyalty.

Personas Development Process in B2B:

1. Research: Collecting data through surveys, customer interviews, market analysis and sales feedback.

2. Pattern Identification: Identification of patterns and trends in the data collected to group companies with similar characteristics.

3. Creation of Personas: Creation of detailed personas, including fictitious name, demographic details, challenges, goals and preferences.

4. Validation: Validating personas with sales and customer service teams to ensure they are accurate and representative.

5. Use in Strategies: Personas are used to guide all marketing strategies, from content creation to campaign development.

Practical example:

A company that sells B2B project management software might create a persona called "Professional Project Manager." This persona may have details about their responsibilities, challenges faced in project management, how to deal with budgets and deadlines, and their preferences when seeking software solutions.

Developing personas in B2B marketing is a strategy that allows for a deeper understanding of target companies' needs and helps personalize marketing strategies in a meaningful way. This results in more relevant communications, stronger connections, and ultimately more successful customer relationships.

2.3 Creating relevant content for companies

Creating relevant content plays a key role in Business-to-Business (B2B) marketing, enabling companies to build authority, trust, and lasting relationships with their target companies. In B2B, where purchasing decisions are often complex and based on specific needs, educational, informative and useful content plays a crucial role. Here are the key points that highlight the importance of creating relevant content in B2B marketing:

Building Authority and Trust:

Creating high-quality, relevant content establishes your company as a trusted source of information. By providing valuable insights and solutions to the challenges target companies face, the company demonstrates its knowledge and experience, which builds authority and generates trust.

Response to Specific Needs:

B2B companies often have specific and complex needs. Relevant content addresses these needs in a targeted way, offering tailored solutions that solve real problems faced by the target audience.

Education and Information:

Educational content helps target companies better understand the problems they face and the solutions available. This not only establishes the company as a valued partner, but also helps facilitate informed decision-making by buyers.

Encouraging Engagement:

Relevant content attracts attention and engagement from target companies. This can occur through blogs, whitepapers, videos, webinars and other formats, creating opportunities for interaction and dialogue.

Customization of Strategies:

Creating relevant content allows companies to customize their marketing strategies to meet the needs of each customer segment. This helps target the right messages to the right audience, increasing the effectiveness of campaigns.

Stand Out in a Competitive Market:

In a competitive B2B market, creating differentiated content can make a difference. Content that offers unique insights, addresses relevant topics, and delivers real value is more likely to stand out and attract the attention of target companies.

Developing Lasting Relationships:

By consistently providing relevant content, companies can nurture relationships over time. This is crucial for B2B sales, where cycles can be longer and trust is key.

Practical example:

A company offering industrial automation solutions might create content such as whitepapers on how to optimize production processes, tutorial videos on configuring their solutions, and webinars discussing industry trends. This content provides valuable knowledge and helps build trust with potential customers.

Creating relevant content in B2B marketing is an essential strategy for educating, engaging and building relationships with target companies. Customized content that addresses specific needs demonstrates a company's commitment to solving problems and offering effective solutions, laying a solid foundation for business success.

2.4 Influencer marketing in B2B

Influencer marketing, traditionally associated with the B2C market, has also played a growing and valuable role in the Business-to-Business (B2B) context. It is a strategy where companies collaborate with opinion leaders, industry experts and other influential professionals to promote their products or services to target companies. Here are the key points about influencer marketing in the B2B context:

Impact of Expert Collaboration:

Partnering with thought leaders and industry experts in B2B can have a significant impact on the perception and trust of target companies. These experts are seen as reliable sources of information and knowledge. When they endorse or recommend B2B products or services, it can validate the quality and relevance of those offerings in the eyes of potential customers.

Building Trusting Relationships:

In B2B, where purchasing decisions tend to be more complex and based on trust, collaborating with influencers can help companies build strong, lasting relationships. The endorsement of a recognized expert can facilitate decision-making for purchasing companies.

Access to Segmented Audiences:

Industry influencers have specific followers and audiences. Collaborating with them allows B2B companies to directly reach the audiences that are most relevant to their products or services, ensuring their messages reach the right people.

Differences between B2B and B2C Influencer Marketing:

1. Tone and Content: In B2B, content is more focused on detailed information and practical solutions, as buying companies are interested in clear benefits for their business. In B2C, content can be more emotional and experience-based.

2. Long-Term Relationships: In B2B, influencer partnerships are often long-term. Developing lasting relationships is crucial to building trust and credibility.

3. Precise Targeting: B2B audiences are more segmented, so the influencers chosen need to be relevant to specific sectors or industry niches.

4. Focus on Solutions: In B2B, the focus is on the solutions that products or services can offer to improve the business of buying companies, while in B2C, the emphasis may be more on convenience or lifestyle.

Practical example:

A company that offers software solutions for B2B supply chain management can collaborate with a recognized influencer in the field of logistics and operations. This influencer can share insights into the benefits of software to optimize processes and improve supply chain efficiency.

Influencer marketing in B2B involves strategic collaboration with industry experts to promote products and services to target companies. This strategy can reinforce trust, build relationships and provide access to highly segmented audiences, while meeting the specific needs of the B2B market.

2.5 Measuring results in B2B campaigns

Measuring results in Business-to-Business (B2B) marketing campaigns is essential to evaluate the success of implemented strategies and make informed decisions for optimization. B2B campaigns often have specific goals, such as qualified lead generation and return on investment (ROI), and key performance indicators (KPIs) are essential for measuring progress toward those goals. Here are the main points that highlight the importance of measuring results in B2B campaigns:

Actual Performance Assessment:

Measurement allows companies to understand the real impact of their campaigns. By tracking specific metrics, you can determine whether goals are being achieved and whether strategies are working as planned.

Focus on B2B Objectives:

B2B-specific KPIs like qualified lead generation, conversions, closed sales, and ROI help measure campaign success in terms of tangible results that drive business growth.

Continuous Optimization:

Metrics analysis provides valuable insights into what is working and what needs to be adjusted. By identifying areas of success and those in need of improvement, companies can optimize their strategies to achieve better results over time.

Data-Driven Adjustments:

Instead of making decisions based on intuition, measuring results allows companies to make informed decisions based on hard data. This reduces the risk of investing resources in strategies that are not producing positive results.

Insights Identification:

Metrics analysis can reveal valuable insights into target audience behavior, the performance of different marketing channels, and customer preferences. This informs future decisions and helps refine marketing approaches.

Investment Justification:

By measuring results, companies can demonstrate the impact of marketing on business growth. This is especially important for management teams and for allocating resources in future campaigns.

Practical example:

Imagine a B2B software company that launches an email marketing campaign to promote its new financial management solution. KPIs would include the open rate of emails, the click rate on links to the landing page, the number of forms completed by interested visitors, and the conversion rate from leads to paying customers. These indicators would help the company evaluate the success of the campaign and identify areas for improvement.

Measuring results in B2B campaigns is essential for evaluating performance, measuring progress towards objectives and optimizing strategies. B2B-specific KPIs enable companies to make informed decisions based on hard data, continually improving return on investment and driving campaign success.

Chapter 3: B2B Sales and Negotiations

3.1 Sales cycle in the B2B environment

The sales cycle in the Business-to-Business (B2B) context refers to the process that companies go through from identifying a potential customer to actually closing the deal. Unlike the Business-to-Consumer (B2C) environment, the B2B sales cycle is generally longer and more complex due to the nature of transactions between companies, which involve more thoughtful and complex decisions. Here are typical stages of the B2B sales cycle:

1. Prospecting:
In this phase, companies identify and qualify potential leads that fit the ideal customer profile. This may involve market research, data analysis and initial contact with companies that have shown interest.

2. Qualification:
After identifying potential leads, companies evaluate them to determine whether they truly have a problem or need that their solution can solve. The qualification helps to focus efforts on the companies most likely to benefit from the offer.

3. Approach and Initial Contact:
At this stage, companies contact qualified leads, usually through emails, phone calls or in-person meetings. The objective is to establish an initial relationship, better understand the needs of the company and present the solution.

4. Presentation and Proposal:
Once interest is confirmed, companies make a detailed presentation of their solution, highlighting how it will meet the specific needs of the purchasing company. This can involve product demonstrations, use case examples, and crafting custom proposals.

5. Negotiation:
At this stage, negotiations take place on contract details, price, terms and conditions. B2B negotiations can be complex due

to the personalized nature of the solutions and the need to align expectations between the parties.

6. Decision Making:

In the B2B sales cycle, multiple stakeholders and decision makers are involved. Decision making is a collaborative process, often involving different departments and hierarchical levels of the organization.

7. Closing the Deal:

Once the terms are agreed upon and all parties agree, the deal closes and the contract is signed. In B2B, this process can take longer due to more complex considerations.

8. Implementation and After-Sales:

After the deal closes, companies need to implement the solution and provide ongoing support. The post-sales phase is crucial to ensure customer satisfaction and build a long-term relationship.

The B2B sales cycle is characterized by its many stages, each with its own complexity and challenges. The more considered nature of B2B decisions, detailed negotiations and multiple parties involved contribute to a longer sales cycle aimed at building long-term relationships.

3.2 Consultative sales approaches

Consultative sales approaches play a crucial role in the Business-to-Business (B2B) context by allowing companies to build solid and lasting relationships with their customers, based on a deep understanding of needs and offering personalized solutions. By adopting a consultative approach, companies position themselves as trusted partners focused on providing real value and solving specific problems for client companies. Here are the key points that highlight consultative sales approaches in B2B:

Understanding Customer Needs:

The consultative approach begins with exploring the client company's needs and challenges. This involves asking detailed questions, listening carefully, and understanding the company's current situation to identify opportunities for improvement.

Focus on Solutions:

Once the client's needs are understood, consultative firms focus on offering tailored solutions. This may involve adapting

existing products or services, creating custom solutions, or combining different offerings to meet specific customer needs.
Value Communication:

Instead of simply presenting products, the consultative approach highlights how the proposed solution adds value to the client company. This involves communicating how the solution will solve problems, improve efficiency, save resources or drive growth.
Building Trust:

The consultative approach is based on building trust and strong relationships. By demonstrating a genuine commitment to the client's interests and offering valuable guidance, consultative firms establish a solid foundation for ongoing collaboration.
Long Term Partnership:

The goal of consultative sales is not just to close a one-time deal, but to establish a long-term partnership. This involves a willingness to track solution implementation, provide ongoing support, and adjust offerings as needs evolve.
Positioning as a Specialist:

Consultative sales approaches involve positioning yourself as experts in the area in which the company operates. This is achieved by providing insights, sharing relevant knowledge and offering informed guidance.
Practical example:

Imagine an IT consulting company that takes a consultative approach. Instead of just selling software solutions, it focuses on understanding the specific challenges a company faces. Based on this understanding, she recommends a customized combination of software, training, and technical support to meet the customer's unique needs.

Consultative sales approaches in B2B are essential for building trusting relationships and offering solutions that add real value to client companies. By deeply understanding client needs and proposing personalized solutions, consultancy firms stand out as valuable partners and contribute to the long-term success of their clients.

3.3 Building long-term relationships

Building long-term relationships plays a key role in the Business-to-Business (B2B) environment, allowing companies to establish long-lasting, mutually beneficial partnerships. In B2B, where transactions are often more complex and involve thoughtful decisions, trust and credibility are vital for building solid relationships. Here are the key points that highlight the importance of building long-term relationships in B2B:

Trust and Credibility:

Long-term relationships are based on mutual trust and credibility. Buying companies need to trust that suppliers will keep their promises and deliver high-quality products and services consistently.

Reduction of Perceived Risk:

In B2B, transactions often involve significant financial and operational risks. Long-term relationships help reduce perceived risk as companies have a proven track record of success working together.

Deep Understanding:

The longer the relationship, the greater the understanding companies have of each other. This allows solutions to be more personalized, communications more effective and decisions more aligned with the goals and values of both parties.

Strategic Partnerships:

Long-term relationships often evolve into strategic partnerships, where companies are not just suppliers and buyers, but collaborators seeking mutual growth. These partnerships can result in joint innovation, new product development and expansion opportunities.

Reduction of Acquisition Costs:

Acquiring new customers is generally more expensive than retaining existing customers. Building long-term relationships allows companies to save resources, as they do not need to invest as much in acquiring new customers.

Recommendations and References:

Satisfied customers in long-term relationships are more likely to make recommendations and provide positive references to other companies. This can generate new business and expand your contact network.

Sustainable Growth:

Maintaining long-term relationships contributes to the sustainable growth of companies. Satisfied customers tend to make repeat purchases, in addition to being more open to trying new products or services launched by companies.

Practical example:

A technology company that provides IT consulting services can build long-term relationships with its clients, assisting them in implementing solutions and providing ongoing support over the years. This approach not only contributes to customer satisfaction, but also creates opportunities for future projects and recommendations.

Building long-term relationships in B2B is crucial to establishing solid, trustworthy and mutually beneficial partnerships. The trust and credibility cultivated in these relationships are fundamental to the sustainable growth of companies, allowing collaboration, innovation and continuous expansion.

3.4 Effective negotiation tactics in B2B

Effective negotiation tactics in the Business-to-Business (B2B) context are essential for reaching mutually beneficial agreements and building strong customer relationships. The complex nature of B2B transactions requires strategic approaches that go beyond simply closing deals. Here are the top effective negotiation tactics in B2B:

Creating Mutual Value:

Rather than focusing solely on price, B2B negotiations should focus on creating mutual value. This involves identifying opportunities for both parties to obtain additional benefits beyond the product or service in question. By finding ways to meet the needs and goals of both parties, negotiation becomes more advantageous.

Identification of Leverage Points:

Understanding leverage points is crucial to directing negotiations effectively. This involves identifying the aspects that are most important to the other party and using these points as a basis for negotiations. Points of leverage may include tight deadlines, unique requirements, or competitive advantages.

Solution Based Negotiation:

An effective approach is solutions-based negotiation, where both parties work together to resolve problems or overcome challenges. Rather than viewing negotiation as a contest for position, this approach seeks to find creative ways to meet the needs of both parties.

Deep Understanding of Customer Needs:

Successful negotiation starts with a deep understanding of the client's needs, goals and challenges. The more the selling company understands the specific needs of the buying company, the more effective the negotiation will be in offering tailored solutions.

Focus on Benefits, Not Features:

When communicating the value of your offer, it is important to highlight the benefits it will provide to the purchasing company. This involves linking your offer to the buying company's goals and objectives, rather than just listing the features of the product or service.

Preparation and Research:

Effective negotiation requires careful preparation and research. This includes knowing the purchasing company, its competitors, the sector in which they operate and their main concerns and challenges.

Active Listening:

During negotiations, active listening is essential. This involves listening carefully to what the other party is saying, understanding their concerns, and responding appropriately. Active listening demonstrates respect and helps identify opportunities to reach a satisfactory agreement.

Practical example:

Imagine a company that sells industrial automation equipment. During negotiations with a manufacturing company, she discovers that the customer is looking to reduce operating costs and increase efficiency. The selling company can adapt its proposal to highlight how its equipment will help achieve these objectives, creating mutual value.

Effective negotiation tactics in B2B involve creating mutual value, identifying leverage points, and solutions-based negotiation. In-depth understanding of client needs, careful preparation and a collaborative approach are key to ensuring that negotiations are successful and lead to win-win agreements.

3.5 After-sales management and customer loyalty

After-sales management plays a crucial role in the Business-to-Business (B2B) environment, enabling companies to maintain customer satisfaction, build strong relationships and achieve long-term success. In B2B, where transactions are often more complex and solutions have a significant impact on customers' businesses, ongoing post-sale support is essential to ensure expectations are met and partnerships are maintained. Here are the main points that highlight the importance of after-sales management and customer loyalty in B2B:

Maintaining Customer Satisfaction:

After-sales management involves continuing the customer relationship after the initial sale. This includes providing technical support, training, assistance and troubleshooting. Ongoing support contributes to customer satisfaction by demonstrating a long-term commitment to ensuring the solution works as expected.

Solution Value Maximization:

Through after-sales management, companies can help customers make the most of their solution. This involves offering training to ensure users are using all features effectively and providing guidance on how to optimize the results achieved with the solution.

Building Lasting Relationships:

Ongoing support after the sale helps build lasting relationships. Companies that demonstrate a genuine interest in helping their customers succeed strengthen bonds and build trust over time.

Churn Reduction (Cancellation Rate):

After-sales management plays an important role in reducing the cancellation rate. Satisfied, well-served customers are less likely to look for alternatives and more likely to continue purchasing and using the company's products or services.

Contribution to Recurring Revenue:

Customer loyalty in B2B contributes to recurring revenue. Satisfied and loyal customers tend to renew contracts, make additional purchases and even recommend the company to other potential customers.

References and Recommendations:

Satisfied customers are more likely to make recommendations and provide positive references to other businesses. This can generate new business and expand your customer base.

Valuable Feedback:

Ongoing after-sales support allows companies to obtain valuable feedback from customers about the performance of their

products or services. This helps identify areas for improvement and enhancement, allowing for continuous evolution of offerings.
Practical example:
A company that sells B2B project management software offers initial training to its customers after the sale. Additionally, it provides ongoing technical support and regular updates to ensure the software is always meeting the customer's evolving needs. This approach helps the company maintain customer satisfaction and build a long-term relationship.
After-sales management is fundamental to customer satisfaction and long-term success in B2B. Continuous support after the sale, building lasting relationships and customer loyalty contribute to recurring revenue, reduced churn and sustainable growth for companies.

Chapter 4: B2B Platforms and Technologies

4.1 B2B e-commerce platforms

B2B e-commerce platforms are online systems designed specifically to facilitate transactions between companies in the Business-to-Business (B2B) environment. These platforms play a crucial role in simplifying and automating the buying and selling process between companies, providing an efficient and personalized experience. Here are the main points that highlight B2B e-commerce platforms and their differences from B2C:
B2B Transaction Facilitation:
B2B e-commerce platforms are designed to meet the specific needs of businesses, such as making large-volume purchases, negotiating personalized prices, and managing complex orders. They offer an effective way to connect suppliers and buyers, streamlining the process of purchasing products or services.
Customized Catalogs:
Unlike B2C e-commerce platforms, which generally have a single catalog for all consumers, B2B platforms offer personalized catalogs. This allows suppliers to display specific products to

different customers, taking into account commercial agreements, purchasing history and individual preferences.

Custom Quotes and Pricing:

B2B platforms often include custom quoting and pricing features. Buyers can request quotes for large volumes of products or for customized products, and suppliers can respond with prices tailored to specific needs.

Bulk Orders:

In the B2B environment, transactions often involve large volume orders. B2B e-commerce platforms are designed to handle these orders, allowing shoppers to add multiple items to their shopping carts and complete transactions involving larger quantities.

Business Account Management:

B2B e-commerce platforms often allow the creation of business customer accounts, where users can have different levels of access and authorization. This is useful for companies that need to manage multiple people within their organization who may make purchases.

Integration with Internal Systems:

Due to the complex nature of B2B operations, B2B e-commerce platforms can be integrated with companies' internal systems, such as inventory management systems, customer relationship management (CRM) systems, and order management systems.

Focus on Relationships:

B2B platforms often emphasize building long-term relationships. They can offer purchase history tracking capabilities, personalized recommendations, and targeted communications to improve customer service.

Practical example:

A B2B e-commerce platform for office supply sourcing allows a business to purchase products such as paper, pens, and office supplies in large volume. Prices are customized based on quantity purchased, and quote features allow the company to negotiate specific terms before making a purchase.

B2B e-commerce platforms play an essential role in facilitating transactions between companies, offering customized features to meet the complexities of the B2B environment. By enabling custom catalogs, quotes, high-volume orders, and integration with internal systems, these platforms improve the efficiency and effectiveness of B2B transactions.

4.2 Systems integration and automation

Systems integration and automation play a fundamental role in the Business-to-Business (B2B) environment, providing significant advantages to companies by streamlining processes, avoiding rework and improving operational efficiency. In the B2B scenario, where transactions are often complex and involve multiple trading partners, the ability to integrate systems and automate tasks is essential to ensure smooth and efficient operations. Here are the key points that highlight the importance of systems integration and automation in B2B:

Process Streamlining:

Systems integration enables the rapid and accurate exchange of information between different parts of the business process. This eliminates the need for manual data entry and reduces reliance on slow, error-prone communications. As a result, processes run more efficiently and with fewer delays.

Avoid Rework:

Systems integration reduces the risk of rework as data is automatically shared between relevant systems. This eliminates the need to repeatedly enter the same data into multiple systems and reduces the likelihood of human errors resulting from manual entry.

Improving Operational Efficiency:

Automating routine tasks and integrating processes allows companies to increase their operational efficiency. Tasks such as order processing, invoicing, inventory management and delivery tracking can be automated, freeing up resources for more strategic activities.

Real-Time Information Flow:

Systems integration allows information to flow in real time between parties involved in a B2B transaction. This provides real-time visibility into the status of orders, inventories, payments and other critical activities, enabling more informed decision-making.

Error Reduction:

Automation and integration significantly reduce human errors, which can occur when manually entering data into different systems. This results in greater precision in processes and less need for subsequent corrections.

Improving Customer Experience:

Systems integration can lead to improved customer experience as customers can receive real-time updates on their orders and have complete visibility into their purchase and transaction histories.

Efficient Business Partner Management:

Systems integration facilitates communication and collaboration with business partners such as suppliers and distributors. This leads to more efficient supply chain management and smoother coordination of operations.

Practical example:

A manufacturing company that integrates its inventory management system with a distributor's order management system can automate the inventory replenishment process. When stock levels reach a minimum threshold, an order is automatically generated and sent to the distributor, speeding replenishment and avoiding product shortages.

Systems integration and automation play a critical role in the B2B environment, enabling companies to achieve greater efficiency, accuracy and agility in their operations. By avoiding rework, improving operational efficiency and promoting the flow of real-time information, companies can increase their competitiveness and provide a more satisfactory experience for their business partners and customers.

4.3 Technologies for supply chain optimization

Supply chain optimization in the Business-to-Business (B2B) environment is essential to ensure efficiency, reduce costs and improve customer satisfaction. The use of advanced technologies plays a crucial role in this process, enabling companies to better manage the flows of products, information and money along the supply chain. Here are the main technologies used to optimize the supply chain in B2B:

Tracking Systems:

Tracking systems enable real-time monitoring of products and assets throughout the entire supply chain. This provides visibility into the location, condition and movement of products, enabling more accurate inventory management, reducing the possibility of losses and delays and improving decision-making.

Data analysis:

Data analysis is essential for identifying patterns, trends and insights throughout the supply chain. By collecting and analyzing data from different points in the chain, companies can identify optimization opportunities, identify bottlenecks, predict demands and improve resource allocation.

Demand Forecast:

Demand forecasting is a technology that uses data analysis and statistical models to estimate future demand for products. This helps companies adjust their inventories, plan production and optimize logistics operations according to seasonal variations and market trends.

RFID (Radio Frequency Identification) technology:

RFID technology allows products to be automatically identified and tracked using tags that emit radio frequency signals. This speeds up inventory counting, improves tracking accuracy and speed, and enables better inventory management.

Process Automation:

Process automation involves the use of systems and technologies to perform repetitive tasks automatically. This can include automating orders, invoicing, inventory management and even manufacturing processes. Automation reduces dependence on manual intervention and increases efficiency.

Blockchain Technology:

Blockchain is a technology that offers a secure and transparent way to record transactions throughout the supply chain. It can be used to track the origin and authenticity of products, ensure data integrity and reduce the risk of fraud.

Supply Chain Management Systems (SCM):

Supply chain management systems are platforms that allow the integration and coordination of all chain activities, from raw material acquisition to delivery to the end customer. These systems help make informed decisions and optimize product and information flows.

Practical example:

A company that manufactures electronic products uses data analytics to forecast demand based on historical sales data and seasonal factors. These forecasts are used to optimize production, ensure components are available at the right time, and avoid stock-outs during demand spikes.

Supply chain optimization technologies in B2B play an essential role in improving logistics efficiency. By using tracking systems, data analysis, demand forecasting and other advanced tools, companies can make more informed decisions, reduce costs and offer a more agile and satisfactory service to their business partners and customers.

4.4 Use of CRM and ERP in a non-B2B environment

The use of CRM (Customer Relationship Management) and ERP (Enterprise Resource Planning) systems offers a series of significant benefits to companies in the Business-to-Business (B2B) environment, helping to improve customer relationship management, automation processes and support informed decision-making. These tools are vital for companies that want to streamline their operations and provide exceptional service to their trading partners. Here are the key points that highlight the benefits of using CRM and ERP in the B2B environment:

CRM (Customer Relationship Management):

1. Customer Relationship Management: CRM allows companies to keep a detailed record of all interactions with their customers. This includes purchase history, preferences, complaints and communications. This visibility helps improve customer service, personalize interactions, and build stronger relationships.

2. Sales and Marketing Automation: CRM automation tools allow you to automate sales and marketing tasks, such as sending emails, tracking leads and scheduling follow-ups. This speeds up processes, improves the efficiency of the sales team and increases the chances of conversion.

3. 360 Degree View of the Customer: CRM offers a holistic view of the customer, bringing together data from various sources. This helps you understand customer needs and preferences, allowing for a more personalized and targeted approach.

4. Improved Customer Retention: With effective relationship management, companies can identify problems and opportunities to improve customer satisfaction. This, in turn, leads to greater customer retention and possible repeat sales.

ERP (Enterprise Resource Planning):

1. Process Automation: ERP systems automate and integrate internal processes, such as inventory management, billing, accounting and human resources. This reduces manual errors, eliminates rework and improves operational efficiency.

2. Integrated Company View: ERP provides a unified view of the company's operations, allowing managers to have detailed insights into different business areas. This makes it easier to identify areas for improvement and make informed decisions.

3. Resource Planning and Control: ERP helps optimize the allocation of resources, from raw materials to workforce. This leads to more effective planning, reduced waste and increased productivity.

4. Strategic Decision Support: With real-time data available, ERP supports strategic decision making. Managers can access key information to evaluate performance, identify trends and align business strategies.

Practical example:

A B2B distribution company uses an ERP system to manage its inventories, purchasing and logistics. The system helps optimize inventory levels, prevent product shortages and improve supply chain efficiency. At the same time, a CRM system is used to track and manage customer orders, ensuring fast and personalized service.

The use of CRM and ERP systems in the B2B environment brings significant benefits, including better customer relationship management, automation of internal processes and insights for strategic decision making. These tools help companies become more efficient, competitive and customer-oriented in an increasingly complex B2B landscape.

4.5 Cybersecurity and data protection in B2B

Cybersecurity and data protection are critical issues in the Business-to-Business (B2B) environment, where companies share sensitive and confidential information throughout the supply chain. The increasing digitization and interconnection between companies has increased exposure to cyber risks, making it imperative to adopt robust security measures. Here are the key points that highlight the importance of cybersecurity and data protection in B2B:

Risks of Data Leaks:

In B2B, companies share confidential information such as deal details, business agreements, financial information and customer details. Exposing this data to cyber threats, such as hackers and phishing attacks, can result in data leaks that are damaging to companies' reputations and trust.

Financial and Legal Impacts:

Data leaks can have significant financial consequences, including regulatory fines, lawsuits, lost revenue and recovery costs. Additionally, companies can be held liable for not adequately protecting the information of their business partners.

Interruption of Operations:

Successful cyberattacks can disrupt business operations, affecting production, the delivery of products and services, and jeopardizing business continuity.

Reliability and Trust:

Cybersecurity is essential to establishing and maintaining reliability and trust between business partners. Companies that demonstrate a solid commitment to data protection are more likely to be chosen as partners.

Robust Security Measures:

Companies can adopt several security measures to protect their data and that of their partners:

1. Data Encryption: Encryption ensures that data is transmitted and stored securely, making it inaccessible to unauthorized persons.

2. Restricted Access: Implementing strict access controls ensures that only authorized persons can access confidential information.

3. Network Monitoring: Monitoring the network for suspicious activity can help identify cyber threats before they cause significant damage.

4. Awareness Training: Providing employees with cybersecurity training helps prevent insider threats and promotes a culture of security.

5. Software Updates: Keeping systems and software updated with the latest security patches helps mitigate known vulnerabilities.

6. Data Backup: Regularly backing up critical data ensures recovery in case of ransomware attacks or data loss.

Practical example:

A B2B manufacturing company implements a restricted access policy to its order management systems and financial information. Additionally, it conducts periodic cybersecurity awareness training for all employees, teaching them how to identify and avoid threats.

Cybersecurity and data protection are critical in the B2B environment to protect sensitive information, prevent data leaks and maintain trust between trading partners. Adopting robust security measures is crucial to mitigating risks, protecting the company's reputation and ensuring continuity of operations.

Chapter 5: B2B Logistics and Supply Chain

5.1 Logistics and distribution in B2B

Logistics and distribution play a vital role in the Business-to-Business (B2B) environment, where efficient delivery of products between companies is crucial to ensuring customer satisfaction, maintaining competitiveness and facilitating smooth running of operations. In B2B, the complexity of products, the scale of transactions and the interconnected nature of the supply chain make logistics an essential part of the process. Here are the main points that highlight the importance of logistics and distribution in B2B:

Efficient Product Delivery:

Product delivery in B2B is often complex, involving products of different sizes, weights and characteristics. Additionally, companies may have specific delivery requirements, such as scheduled times, partial deliveries, and variable demands.

Route Optimization:

Route optimization is essential to reduce costs and improve distribution efficiency. This involves calculating the shortest and most effective routes to deliver products to destinations, minimizing transit time and operational costs.

Process Coordination:

Logistics in B2B requires careful coordination between different parts of the supply chain, including suppliers, carriers, warehouses and customers. Effective communication and collaboration are key to ensuring products move efficiently throughout the chain.

Stock Management:

Logistics in B2B also includes inventory management, ensuring that products are available when needed. This involves predicting demand, carrying out timely replenishments and avoiding shortages or excess stock.

Customer Experience:

On-time and efficient delivery is crucial to customer satisfaction in B2B. Companies that can meet delivery deadlines and offer a seamless delivery experience earn customers' trust and loyalty.

Technology in Logistics:

Advanced technologies such as real-time tracking systems, data analytics and automation play an important role in optimizing B2B logistics. These tools allow you to monitor the progress of shipments, make informed decisions based on data, and automate repetitive tasks.

Practical example:

A B2B electronics distribution company uses a real-time tracking system to monitor the location and status of shipments in transit. This allows them to quickly identify any delays or issues and proactively communicate with customers about the status of their deliveries.

Logistics and distribution are critical components in the B2B environment, where efficient delivery of products between companies is fundamental. Route optimization, process coordination and the use of advanced technologies help ensure distribution efficiency and customer satisfaction, contributing to the overall success of B2B operations.

5.2 Inventory and demand management

Inventory and demand management plays a crucial role in the Business-to-Business (B2B) supply chain, enabling companies to balance product availability to meet customer demand while avoiding excessive inventories or shortages. This efficient approach is essential to ensure continuity of operations, reduce costs and increase customer satisfaction. Here are the key points that highlight the role of inventory and demand management in the B2B environment:

Inventory Level Optimization:

Inventory management involves determining the ideal level of inventory a company should maintain to meet demand. This requires a delicate balance to avoid situations where inventory is either too low, leading to product shortages, or too high, resulting in additional storage costs.

Demand Forecast:

Demand forecasting is a key component of inventory management. It involves analyzing historical data, market trends, seasonality and other factors to estimate the quantity of products that will be needed in a given period. These forecasts help companies prepare adequately to meet future demand.

Just-in-Time (JIT) and Safety Stock:

In B2B, the Just-in-Time (JIT) approach is common, where companies seek to maintain minimum inventories, receiving products when they are needed to avoid overstocking. However, it is also important to consider a safety stock to deal with variations in demand and possible delays in the supply chain.

Use of Technology and Data Analysis:

Advanced technologies such as inventory management systems and data analytics play a vital role in effectively managing inventory and demand. These tools allow you to monitor the flow of products, identify demand patterns, calculate ideal inventory levels, and adjust strategies accordingly.

Collaboration with Suppliers:

Collaboration with suppliers is essential for effective inventory and demand management. Transparent communication and information sharing help align expectations and avoid discrepancies between supply and demand.

Practical example:

A B2B food company that supplies ingredients to restaurants uses an inventory management system connected to its customers' systems. When a customer's stock levels reach a pre-defined replenishment point, the system automatically generates a replenishment order, ensuring ingredients are available when needed.

Inventory and demand management is essential in the B2B supply chain to balance product supply and demand. Through demand forecasting, use of technology and effective collaboration, companies can avoid overstocks and shortages, ensuring continuity of operations and customer satisfaction.

5.3 Transport and freight strategies

Transportation and freight strategies play an essential role in Business-to-Business (B2B) supply chain efficiency, enabling companies to quickly, cost-effectively and reliably deliver products to their trading partners. Choosing the appropriate mode of transport and forming solid partnerships with transport companies are strategic decisions that directly affect the success of operations. Here are the main points that highlight transportation and freight strategies in B2B:

Modes of Transportation:

There are several modes of transport available, such as road, rail, sea and air. The choice of mode of transport depends on several factors, such as distance, required speed, nature of products, costs and delivery requirements. For example, perishable products may require air transport for quick delivery, while bulk goods may be better suited for sea transport.

Efficiency versus Cost:

The choice of transport mode must balance efficiency and cost. Air transport is fast but generally more expensive. Shipping by sea is economical but can be slower. Understanding customer needs and market demands is crucial to finding the right balance between these factors.

Partnerships with Carriers:

Partnerships with reliable and experienced carriers are essential to ensure consistent and punctual deliveries. Choosing partners that meet quality standards and offer real-time tracking can increase supply chain reliability.

Reverse logistic:

In B2B, reverse logistics is also important. This involves returning unsold products, defective parts or customer returns. An effective reverse logistics strategy can reduce costs, minimize environmental impact and improve customer satisfaction.

Technology and Tracking:

Technology plays a crucial role in monitoring and tracking shipments. Real-time tracking systems allow companies and their customers to track the status of deliveries, identifying the location and estimated time of arrival.

Practical example:

A B2B electronics company chooses to use trucking to deliver its products to retailers across the country. They partner with a carrier that offers real-time tracking, allowing retailers to track deliveries and plan their operations accordingly.

Transportation and freight strategies are vital to B2B supply chain efficiency. Choosing the appropriate mode of transportation, establishing reliable partnerships, and using tracking technology are essential components to ensuring successful deliveries and customer satisfaction throughout the supply chain.

5.4 Partnerships in the B2B supply chain

Partnerships in the Business-to-Business (B2B) supply chain play a crucial role in the success of operations and delivery of customer value. Effective collaboration between suppliers, distributors and other stakeholders creates an environment where companies can leverage synergies, share resources and streamline processes to achieve common goals. Here are the key points that highlight the importance of B2B supply chain partnerships:
Sharing of Knowledge and Experience:
Supply chain partners bring distinct experiences and expertise to the table. Collaboration allows companies to leverage this diversity to solve problems, identify opportunities and learn from each other.
Operational efficiency:
Effective collaboration helps optimize operational processes throughout the supply chain. For example, sharing information about demand and production planning can allow activities to be synchronized, avoiding excessive stocks or shortages.
Response to Market Changes:
Flexible supply chain partnerships allow companies to respond quickly to changes in the market. Whether in situations of sudden increase in demand or changes in customer preferences, partnerships allow for agile adaptation.
Joint Innovation:
Collaborating with partners can lead to joint innovations. Sharing different ideas and perspectives can lead to the development of improved products, more efficient processes, and creative solutions to complex challenges.
Delivering Value to the Customer:
Collaboration along the supply chain enables the delivery of value to the end customer. This is when companies are able to offer high quality products, competitive prices and reliable delivery times, creating a positive customer experience.
Risk management:
Supply chain partners can share responsibilities and mitigate risks. If a supplier faces a production issue, for example,

collaboration can help find workarounds to avoid disruption to operations.
Practical example:

A B2B car manufacturer collaborates closely with its parts suppliers. They share demand forecast and production scheduling data, allowing suppliers to prepare in advance to meet the automaker's needs. This results in on-time deliveries, reduced costs and more efficient production.

Partnerships in the B2B supply chain are fundamental to the success of operations and the delivery of value to the customer. Collaboration between suppliers, distributors and other stakeholders promotes operational efficiency, resilience and innovation, enabling companies to more effectively meet market challenges and offer high quality products and services to their customers.

5.5 Sustainability and social responsibility in B2B logistics

Sustainability and social responsibility are playing an increasingly important role in Business-to-Business (B2B) logistics, as companies recognize the importance of minimizing their environmental impact and making a positive contribution to the communities in which they operate. Logistics, as an integral part of the supply chain, plays a key role in implementing these sustainable practices. Here are the key points that highlight the role of sustainability and social responsibility in B2B logistics:
Emissions Reduction and Environmental Impact:

Companies are adopting logistics practices that minimize carbon emissions and reduce environmental impact. This can include optimizing routes to reduce the distance travelled, using low-emission vehicles and looking for more sustainable modes of transport such as rail and sea transport.
Energy Efficiency:

The quest for energy efficiency is driving the adoption of more fuel-efficient vehicles and equipment. In addition, companies are investing in fleet monitoring and management technologies to reduce energy consumption and optimize the use of resources.
Sustainable Packaging:

Choosing sustainable packaging is a growing concern in B2B logistics. Companies are opting for recyclable, reusable or low environmental impact packaging to reduce waste and pollution.
Responsible Disposal Practices:
In addition to considering the transportation phase, companies are focusing on responsible disposal practices. This involves the appropriate management of waste and discarded materials, avoiding environmental contamination.
Social Responsibility in the Supply Chain:
Social responsibility also extends to labor practices and the promotion of well-being in logistics operations. Companies are ensuring that workers involved in the supply chain are treated fairly and safely.
Transparency and Traceability:
Companies are embracing greater supply chain transparency, tracing the origin of products and ensuring that suppliers meet ethical and sustainable standards.
Practical example:
A B2B electronics company chooses to use packaging made from recyclable and biodegradable materials for its products. In addition, they contract with carriers that own fleets of electric vehicles and partner with suppliers that adopt ethical work practices.
Sustainability and social responsibility are gaining prominence in B2B logistics, with companies adopting practices that minimize environmental impact and contribute to the well-being of communities. These approaches not only benefit the planet and people, but can also result in more efficient operations and a positive image for companies along the supply chain.

Chapter 6: Pricing and B2B Contracts

6.1 Pricing models in B2B

In the Business-to-Business (B2B) context, several pricing models are used to determine the value of products or services offered. Each model aims to meet the needs of companies effectively, considering factors such as costs, perceived value and market dynamics. Here are the main pricing models in B2B:

Cost-Based Pricing:

In this model, prices are defined based on production, distribution and operational costs, plus a profit margin. This model is simpler to calculate and can be suitable for products or services with well-defined costs. However, it does not take into account external factors such as demand or the value perceived by the customer.

Pricing Based on Perceived Value:

In this model, prices are determined based on the value that customers perceive in relation to the product or service. Companies seek to understand the problems their customers are trying to solve and assign a price based on the savings or benefit the customer will receive from purchasing the product. This allows companies to capture a portion of the value they generate for their customers.

Dynamic Pricing:

Dynamic pricing involves adjusting prices according to demand and other factors in real time. This may include higher prices during periods of high demand or lower prices during periods of low demand. Technology plays an important role in this model, allowing companies to monitor and readjust prices quickly.

Pricing by Tiers or Segments:

In this model, products or services are offered at different levels or segments with corresponding prices. Each tier may offer different features, functionality, or levels of support. This allows companies to serve different customer segments with different needs and budgets.

Subscription or Access Pricing:

This model involves the regular payment of a fixed fee to access a product or service for a certain period. It's common in industries like software, where customers pay monthly or annually to use a service or platform.

Negotiated Pricing:

In many B2B scenarios, prices are negotiated directly between the supplier and the customer. This may involve customized arrangements based on specific customer needs and volumes.

Results-Based Pricing:

Some pricing models are directly linked to the results achieved for the client. This may involve paying based on specific goals or performance achieved, as with digital marketing services.

Practical example:

A B2B software company may offer different levels of subscription plans based on the amount of features, support, and advanced functionality. Customers can choose the plan that best suits their needs and budget.

Different pricing models are applied in the B2B context, depending on product characteristics, market dynamics and customer needs. Choosing the right model is essential to ensure the company captures appropriate value, is competitive in the market and meets the expectations of business customers.

6.2 Considerations in price formation

Pricing in the Business-to-Business (B2B) environment is a complex task that requires the consideration of several factors to ensure that prices are competitive, aligned with the value perceived by customers and sustainable for the company. Here are the key considerations in B2B pricing:

1. Costs:

Production, distribution and operating costs are the basis for many B2B pricing strategies. Prices need to cover these costs and, ideally, provide profit margins that allow the company to continue investing and growing.

2. Competition:

Analyzing the competition is crucial to understanding how your prices stack up against the market. Prices that are too high can drive customers away, while prices that are too low can hurt profitability. It's important to strike a balance that reflects your company's value proposition.

3. Added Value:

The customer's perceived value is a key element in B2B pricing. Customers are willing to pay more for products or services that offer superior value. It's important to clearly communicate the added value your product or service offers over competing solutions.

4. Market Strategies:

Market strategy plays a significant role in price formation. A cost leadership approach can lead to lower prices to attract a broad customer base, while a differentiation strategy can justify higher prices based on unique features and superior quality.

5. Elasticity of Demand:

The elasticity of demand measures the sensitivity of customers to price changes. If demand is elastic, a small change in price can lead to large changes in quantity demanded. Understanding demand elasticity helps you determine how to adjust prices to optimize revenue.

6. Economic Scenario:

The economic environment also plays a role in price formation. In periods of economic growth, companies may be more willing to pay higher prices for products and services. In times of recession, prices may need to be adjusted to suit customers' price sensitivity.

7. Fixed and Variable Cost Structure:

Understanding the proportion of fixed and variable costs in your products or services is important. If fixed costs are high, you may need to sell a larger quantity to cover these costs. On the other hand, pricing based on variable costs can allow for greater flexibility.

8. Launch Strategies and Product Life Cycle:

During the product lifecycle, prices may be adjusted as the product matures or new versions are released. Higher initial prices can be used to recoup initial investments, while lower prices can be adopted to gain market share.

Practical example:

A B2B company that offers management software decides to adopt a pricing strategy based on perceived value. They identify that their solutions offer time savings, operational efficiency and increased productivity for their customers. They set their prices according to the tangible benefits customers get from using the software.

Pricing in the B2B environment requires a strategic approach that takes into account costs, competition, added value, market strategies and other relevant factors. Finding the right balance between these elements is critical to maximizing revenue, meeting customer needs and maintaining the company's financial sustainability.

6.3 Negotiation of B2B contracts

Contract negotiation in the Business-to-Business (B2B) context plays a fundamental role in defining the terms and conditions of commercial transactions between companies. It is an essential process for establishing mutually beneficial agreements, ensuring that both parties understand and agree to the expectations, responsibilities and benefits involved. Here are the key points about the importance of B2B contract negotiation:

Establishing Clear Terms:

Contract negotiation allows companies to establish clear and specific terms for their transactions. This includes details such as price, quantity, delivery time, party responsibilities, warranties, return policies, and more. Clear terms avoid future misunderstandings.

Protection of Interests:

Contract negotiation is an opportunity for companies to protect their interests and mitigate risks. By discussing and agreeing on aspects such as liability for damages, termination clauses and limitations of liability, the parties can avoid disputes and litigation in the future.

Customization:

Each B2B contract can be customized to meet the specific needs of the parties involved. This includes considerations such as unique products or services, purchase volumes, payment terms, and other details that vary by business.

Negotiation Process Steps:

The B2B contract negotiation process generally includes steps such as preparation, initial discussions, exchange of proposals, counter-proposals, legal reviews, finalization and signing. Each step involves communication, information exchange and decision making.

Effective Trading Strategies:

Effective negotiation strategies include identifying common interests, listening carefully to the other party's concerns, seeking creative solutions, focusing on mutually beneficial outcomes, and being flexible in pursuit of an equitable agreement.

Communication and Relationship:

Open and transparent communication is essential when negotiating B2B contracts. Building a trusting relationship helps to overcome impasses, resolve differences and reach an agreement that suits both parties.

Balance between Competitiveness and Collaboration:

Although negotiation involves seeking advantages, the focus should also be on building a long-term relationship. Striking a balance between competitiveness and collaboration is important to ensure that both parties benefit.

Practical example:

An electronics manufacturer is negotiating a supply contract with a component supplier. During negotiations, both parties discuss prices, volumes, delivery times and quality clauses. They agree on terms that reflect the needs of both parties, establishing a solid foundation for a successful business relationship.

Contract negotiation in the B2B environment is a critical part of the commercial process, ensuring that transactions occur in a transparent, fair and mutually beneficial manner. Through effective communication, solid negotiation strategies and a focus on building relationships, companies can establish agreements that meet their needs and sustain long-term success.

6.4 Key elements in B2B contracts

B2B contracts are legal documents that establish the terms and conditions of business transactions between companies. They are essential to ensure clarity, legality and protection of the interests of both parties involved. Here are the essential elements that must be present in B2B contracts:

1. Identification of the Parties:

The contract must contain the identifying information of the companies involved, including their names, addresses and contact details.

2. Definition of Products or Services:

A detailed description of the products or services to be provided must be included, including technical specifications, quantities and important characteristics.

3. Prices and Payment Terms:

The contract must establish the agreed prices for the products or services, as well as the payment terms, including payment deadlines and methods.

4. Deadlines and Delivery:

It is important to set clear deadlines for the delivery of products or services. This includes start dates, completion dates, and any interim milestones.

5. Obligations of the Parties:

The contract must detail the obligations and responsibilities of each party involved. This may include responsibilities for delivery, quality, after-sales support and other relevant commitments.

6. Termination Clauses:

Clauses that deal with the termination of the contract are essential to establish the conditions under which one of the parties can terminate the agreement. This may include notice periods, termination conditions for default and other details.

7. Intellectual Property and Copyright:

If the contract involves the creation or transfer of intellectual property, it is important to detail how copyrights, patents and other assets will be treated.

8. Confidentiality and Privacy:

Confidentiality clauses are used to protect sensitive information shared during the course of the business relationship. This includes details about how confidential information will be handled and protected.

9. Limitations of Liability:

The parties may establish limitations on each other's liability in the event of problems or failures. This helps protect companies from excessive claims.

10. Applicable Law and Jurisdiction:

The contract must establish which law will govern the agreement and which jurisdiction will be responsible for resolving any disputes.

11. General Clauses:

In addition to specific elements, B2B contracts may also include general clauses, such as force majeure clauses (which deal with unforeseeable events that prevent performance of the contract) and waiver clauses (which specify that failure to enforce a term does not imply a waiver of this right).

Practical example:

A manufacturing company is negotiating a B2B contract with a raw materials supplier. The contract includes details about the products to be supplied, prices, delivery times, responsibilities of both parties, termination clauses in case of non-compliance and confidentiality agreements to protect sensitive information.

The essential elements present in B2B contracts are designed to ensure clarity, legality and protection of the interests of both parties involved in a commercial transaction. By defining terms, conditions, obligations, and other details precisely and comprehensively, B2B contracts lay a solid foundation for successful business relationships.

6.5 Resolution of contractual conflicts in B2B

Resolving contractual conflicts in the Business-to-Business (B2B) environment is an essential part of maintaining healthy business relationships and avoiding protracted disputes. The complex nature of B2B transactions can lead to disagreements, but there are effective approaches to resolving these conflicts efficiently and fairly. Here are the main aspects related to resolving contractual conflicts in B2B:

Alternative Resolution Methods:

1. Mediation: Mediation involves appointing an impartial third party to help the parties reach an agreement. The mediator facilitates communication, but does not impose decisions. This method is less formal and can preserve the relationship between the parties.

2. Arbitration: Arbitration is a more formal process in which the parties agree to submit the dispute to an arbitrator or panel of arbitrators. The arbitrator's decision is binding, similar to a court ruling, and is often faster and less expensive than litigation in court.

Conflict Prevention Through Contractual Clauses:

1. Mediation and Arbitration Clauses: Parties may include contractual clauses that stipulate that, in the event of a dispute, they undertake to try to resolve the issue through mediation or arbitration before resorting to legal proceedings.

2. Jurisdiction and Governing Law Clauses: Defining jurisdiction and applicable law in the contract can help avoid disputes over where a dispute should be resolved and which law will apply.

3. Termination and Dispute Resolution Clauses: Including detailed clauses that address the termination terms and dispute resolution process can help avoid misunderstandings and provide a clear roadmap for dealing with issues.

Open Communication and Negotiation:

When conflicts arise, open communication and constructive negotiation are essential. Parties involved should seek to resolve issues through direct discussions, sharing concerns and exploring mutually acceptable solutions.

Litigation as Last Resort:

Litigation in court is generally considered the last resort for resolving contractual disputes. It's a time-consuming, expensive process and can damage business relationships. Therefore, it is often preferable to explore alternative methods of resolution before resorting to litigation.

Practical example:

A technology company is in a dispute with a B2B customer over missed delivery deadlines. Both parties agreed to try to resolve the dispute through mediation. A mediator is appointed to facilitate discussions between the parties and help them reach an agreement on the best way to resolve the issue.

Resolving contractual conflicts in the B2B environment is an important part of maintaining healthy relationships and avoiding protracted litigation. Including contract clauses that address dispute resolution, along with consideration of alternative methods such as mediation and arbitration, can help promote efficient and fair dispute resolution.

Chapter 7: Internationalization in the B2B Environment

7.1 Opportunities and challenges of B2B international trade

International trade offers significant opportunities for B2B companies to expand their markets, reach new customers and increase their revenue base. However, it also brings with it a number of challenges that need to be addressed to ensure success in the global environment. Here are the main opportunities and challenges of B2B international trade:

Opportunities:

1. Access to New Markets: International expansion allows companies to access markets that may have growing demand for their products or services, opening up new opportunities for growth.

2. Risk Diversification: By operating in multiple markets, companies can mitigate risks associated with economic and political fluctuations in a single country.

3. Leveraging Unique Resources and Skills: Internationalization can allow companies to capitalize on unique resources and skills

available in other countries, such as specialized labor or specific raw materials.

4. Increased Competitiveness: Participating in international trade can boost innovation and product quality, making companies more competitive globally.

Challenges:

1. Trade and Regulatory Barriers: Different countries have different regulations and trade barriers that can make it difficult to enter and operate in international markets.

2. Cultural and Linguistic Differences: Adapting to cultural and linguistic differences is essential to building solid relationships with customers and partners in different countries.

3. Exchange Rate Volatility: Fluctuations in exchange rates can impact production costs, product prices and the profitability of international operations.

4. Logistics and Supply Chain: Efficiently managing logistics and supply chain across multiple countries can be complex due to transportation challenges, customs regulations and geographic distances.

5. Political and Economic Risks: Political changes, economic instability and conflicts can negatively affect international operations.

6. Global Competition: International expansion also means competing with local companies in foreign markets, which can be challenging.

Practical example:

A US-based electronics manufacturer decides to expand into international markets, including Asia. The company faces challenges such as import tariffs, different technical regulations and the need to adapt to local consumer preferences. However, opportunities include a large growth market in the region and the possibility of revenue diversification.

B2B international trade offers exciting opportunities for expansion and growth, but it also presents complex challenges that require a strategic and adaptive approach. Companies seeking to engage in international trade must be prepared to address issues such as trade barriers, cultural differences and currency risks, while also seeking to capitalize on the competitive advantages that global expansion can offer.

7.2 Cultural and legal adaptation in international transactions

Cultural and legal adaptation plays a key role when transacting across borders in the Business-to-Business (B2B) environment. Globalization offers incredible opportunities, but it also presents unique challenges that companies must face to ensure success and compliance in foreign markets. Here are key points about the importance of cultural and legal adaptation in international transactions:

Cultural Adaptation:

1. Respect for Diversity: Cultural differences impact the way business is conducted, from communication practices to etiquette standards. Respecting and understanding a country's cultural norms is essential to building strong relationships.

2. Effective Communication: Adapting communication to avoid cultural misunderstandings is key. This includes considerations of communication style, tone, language, and even the proper use of gestures and expressions.

3. Negotiation and Decision Making: Different cultures have varying approaches to negotiation and decision making. Some can be more direct, while others value building relationships before discussing business.

Legal Adaptation:

1. Local Regulations and Standards: Each country has specific regulations that may affect a company's operations. This can include rules on imports, exports, taxes, licenses and other business matters.

2. Intellectual Property: Intellectual property laws vary between countries and may affect copyrights, patents, trademarks and trade secrets. Companies need to adequately protect their intellectual property in foreign markets.

3. Contracts and Contract Laws: International contracts must be adapted to reflect local laws, including clauses dealing with jurisdiction and dispute resolution.

4. Workers' Rights: Companies also need to be aware of local labor laws to ensure they are in compliance with employment regulations, benefits and workers' rights.

Issues Related to Intellectual Property:

1. International Registrations: Companies should consider registering their brands, patents and copyrights in countries where they wish to operate to protect their intellectual assets.
2. Respect for the Intellectual Property of Others: Knowing and respecting the intellectual property laws in each country is essential to avoid violations that could result in litigation.
Practical example:

A US fashion company is expanding its operations into the Chinese market. They need to consider adapting their products to suit local preferences and sizes, as well as understanding import regulations and cultural norms of doing business in China.

Cultural and legal adaptation is essential for successful cross-border B2B transactions. Companies that take into account cultural differences, local regulations and intellectual property issues are better prepared to establish successful business relationships and avoid legal conflicts.

7.3 Strategies for entering foreign markets

When entering foreign markets, B2B companies have several strategies at their disposal, each with its specific advantages and challenges. These strategies can be adapted according to the company's objectives, the availability of resources and the characteristics of the target market. Here are some common approaches to global expansion:
1. Direct Export:
Direct exporting involves selling products or services directly to customers or partners in foreign markets. This strategy is suitable for companies looking to start expanding with a low initial investment.
Advantages: Direct control over sales and distribution, lower initial investment, higher profit margin.
Challenges: Need to understand import/export regulations, deal with international logistics, establish local presence.
2. Strategic Partnerships:
Partnerships with local companies can provide access to established distribution networks and market knowledge. These partnerships may include distributors, sales representatives or commercial agents.

Advantages: Leverage local knowledge, reach customers quickly, share risks and costs with partners.

Challenges: Finding reliable partners, aligning goals and interests, ensuring control over the brand and quality.

3. Joint Ventures:

A joint venture involves forming a new entity in partnership with a local business. This can help combine both parties' resources, knowledge and skills to operate in the foreign market.

Advantages: Sharing of resources and risks, direct access to local knowledge and experience, possibility of entering regulated markets.

Challenges: Complexity in managing partnerships, alignment of corporate cultures, potential for conflicts of interest.

4. Acquisitions:

Acquisitions involve buying an existing company in a foreign market. This allows for quick entry and instant access to the customer base and infrastructure.

Advantages: Fast market entry, access to assets and resources, elimination of local competition.

Challenges: Accurate assessment of target company value, integration of cultures and operations, management of acquisition costs.

Practical example:

A US technology company wants to enter the European market. It may opt for a direct export strategy initially, selling its products directly to European customers. As its presence grows, the company may consider strategic partnerships with local distributors to expand its market coverage.

Foreign market entry strategies in the B2B environment should be chosen based on the company's objectives, its resource capacity and the nature of the target market. Each approach has its own advantages and challenges, and the right choice will depend on the specific conditions of each company and market.

7.4 International logistics and global supply chain

The international expansion of B2B companies brings with it significant challenges in terms of logistics and the supply chain. Effective management of these aspects is crucial to ensuring that products are successfully delivered to customers in foreign markets.

Here are the main challenges and logistical considerations involved in international expansion:

1. International Shipping:

Transporting goods across borders involves complex considerations such as choice of transport mode (sea, air, land), import and export regulations, customs costs and transit time. Effective coordination of international transport is essential to avoid delays and ensure on-time deliveries.

2. Inventory Management:

Managing inventory across different geographic locations is a critical challenge. Maintaining the right balance between available stock and foreign market demand is essential to avoid excessive stocks or shortages that could affect operations and customer satisfaction.

3. Supply Chain Coordination:

A global supply chain involves multiple links, from suppliers to end customers. Efficient coordination of all these parties is essential to ensure smooth operations. This can be complicated by distance, time zone and cultural differences.

4. Infrastructure and Local Logistics:

Infrastructure and logistical conditions in each country can vary significantly. The availability of ports, roads, airports and other means of transport will influence the efficiency of transport and distribution.

5. Risk Management:

Risks such as transportation breakdowns, customs delays, political instability and natural disasters can impact the international supply chain. Contingency plans are needed to mitigate these risks.

6. Technology and Tracking:

The use of technology, such as real-time tracking and monitoring systems, is essential for tracking the location and status of shipments in transit, allowing for quick adjustments when necessary.

Importance of Global Operational Efficiency:

Overall operational efficiency is vital to keeping costs under control, ensuring on-time deliveries and meeting customer expectations. This involves optimizing processes, minimizing transit times and maximizing resource utilization.

Practical example:

A US electronic components manufacturer is expanding into Asia. It needs to manage transportation logistics, consider delivery times to different Asian countries, and adapt its inventory to meet varying demands.

The international expansion of B2B companies brings complex challenges in logistics and supply chain management. Global operational efficiency, combined with an understanding of the logistical particularities in different markets, is essential to ensuring that products are delivered effectively and that operations run smoothly on a global level.

7.5 Success stories of internationalized B2B companies

Certainly! Here are some examples of B2B companies that have successfully internationalized and how they faced specific challenges when expanding into foreign markets:

1. IBM:

IBM is a classic example of success in B2B internationalization. As IBM expanded globally, it adapted its strategies to align with local needs and regulations. They have established partnerships with local companies to gain market knowledge and provide technology solutions tailored to the specific needs of each region.

2. Caterpillar:

Caterpillar, a global leader in construction and mining equipment, has had success going international. Upon entering foreign markets, they adjusted their products to meet each country's requirements and also established joint ventures with local partners to improve their presence.

3. Airbnb for Work:

Airbnb has adapted its B2B platform, known as "Airbnb for Work," to meet business travel needs. They have expanded into global markets, adjusting their offerings to accommodate corporate travel and provide convenient accommodations for business travelers.

4. Salesforce:

Salesforce is an example of successful international expansion, offering customer relationship management (CRM) solutions. They addressed challenges like data and privacy regulations, adjusting their platform to comply with local laws and ensure compliance.

5. Zara:

Zara, a Spanish fashion brand, has successfully internationalized by adopting a strategy of rapid supply and localized production. They adjusted their offerings according to the cultural and seasonal preferences of each market, maintaining the freshness of their collections.

6. Maersk:

Maersk, a transportation and logistics company, has expanded globally by building an efficient operations network. They have tackled challenges such as transportation regulations, customs issues and logistics coordination on a global level, investing in infrastructure and technology to overcome these obstacles.

7. Huawei:

Huawei, the Chinese telecommunications giant, has had success internationalizing despite political and regulatory challenges. They have built strategic partnerships and invested in research and development to become a global technology leader.

8. FedEx:

Logistics company FedEx faced regulatory and infrastructure challenges when expanding into foreign markets. They took an adaptive approach, adjusting their operations to deal with local variables and becoming a leading international shipping company.

These examples illustrate how successful internationalizing B2B companies faced unique challenges, adapted their strategies, and addressed the specific needs of each market. Flexibility, understanding local particularities and investment in strategic partnerships and innovation were key factors in its success.

Chapter 8: Future of B2B

8.1 Impact of artificial intelligence on B2B

Artificial intelligence (AI) is playing a transformative role in the Business-to-Business (B2B) sector, revolutionizing the way companies interact, collaborate and conduct business. The impact of AI on B2B is comprehensive and influences several aspects of the operation, from task automation to advanced data analysis. Here are some of the main impacts of AI on the B2B sector:

1. Process Automation:

AI allows for the automation of routine and repetitive tasks, freeing up human resources for more strategic and creative tasks. Processes such as email sorting, customer service via chatbots and order management can be optimized through automation.

2. Advanced Data Analysis:

AI can analyze large volumes of data quickly and accurately, providing valuable insights for strategic decision-making. It can identify patterns, trends and correlations that would be difficult to detect manually.

3. Personalization of the Customer Experience:

AI enables the creation of personalized experiences for customers, offering product recommendations, relevant content and tailored solutions. This helps build stronger, longer-lasting relationships.

4. Supply Chain Optimization:

AI can be used to predict demand, optimize inventory management and improve efficiency in the supply chain, reducing the occurrence of excess stocks or shortages.

5. Decision Assistance:

AI systems can assist in making complex decisions by providing data-driven analyzes and scenarios. This is especially useful for evaluating risks, opportunities and strategic options.

6. Real-Time Monitoring:

AI enables continuous monitoring of data in real-time, helping companies identify operational issues or emerging trends and proactively take corrective action.

7. Marketing and Sales Automation:

In B2B, AI is used to automate marketing activities such as customer segmentation, content personalization, and campaign automation. Additionally, AI can provide insights into qualified leads and help predict sales opportunities.

8. Improving Operational Efficiency:

AI optimizes internal processes, improving efficiency in areas such as project management, resource allocation and operations monitoring.

Practical example:

A B2B logistics company implemented AI systems to optimize delivery routing. AI analyzes factors such as traffic, distances and local restrictions to create more efficient routes, saving time and fuel.

AI is redefining the way B2B companies operate, helping to automate tasks, improve analytics, optimize decisions and increase overall efficiency. Companies that embrace AI are better positioned to compete in an increasingly technological and data-driven business environment.

8.2 Digitization and digital transformation in the B2B sector

Digitization and digital transformation are fundamental concepts that are redefining the way B2B companies operate, interact and conduct business in an increasingly digital environment. These approaches involve the integration and adoption of digital technologies across all areas of a company to drive efficiency, innovation and value creation. Here is a more detailed explanation of these concepts in the B2B context:
Scanning:
Digitization refers to the conversion of processes, activities and information into digital formats, allowing them to be stored, shared and processed more efficiently. It involves replacing manual processes with automated processes and migrating data and information to digital platforms.
Digital Transformation:
Digital transformation goes beyond simple digitization, involving a fundamental change in the way a company operates and creates value. It includes redefining processes, adopting emerging technologies, incorporating advanced data analytics and restructuring business models to meet the demands of a digital world.
Non-B2B Context Impact:
The adoption of digitalization and digital transformation in the B2B sector is generating a series of significant impacts:
1. Innovative Business Models: Digital transformation is enabling the creation of new business models and partnerships, facilitating connections between companies in previously unthinkable ways.
2. Improved Customer Experience: Digitization allows us to offer a more fluid and personalized customer experience, from the purchasing process to after-sales support.

3. Operational Efficiency: Automated and integrated digital processes improve operational efficiency, reducing errors and execution time.

4. Advanced Data Analytics: The ability to collect and analyze large volumes of data helps businesses make informed decisions and identify patterns of customer behavior.

5. New Market Opportunities: Digitalization creates opportunities to explore new markets and segments, often beyond geographic borders.

6. Continuous Innovation: Digital transformation encourages a culture of innovation, allowing companies to test and implement new ideas more quickly.

Practical example:

An industrial equipment manufacturer adopted digital transformation, incorporating IoT (Internet of Things) sensors into its products. These sensors collect real-time data on machine performance, enabling predictive analysis and proactive maintenance, which has improved efficiency and reduced downtime for its B2B customers.

Digitization and digital transformation in the B2B context represent a profound change in the way companies operate, interact and provide value to their customers. The adoption of digital technologies is creating new opportunities, driving efficiency and redefining standards of business excellence.

8.3 Mass customization in B2B commerce

The trend of mass customization in B2B commerce is gaining increasing prominence as companies seek to meet the unique demands of their customers, even in a large-scale sales context. This approach involves using data, technology and intelligent processes to offer customized solutions that meet the specific needs of each client. Here are the main points to consider:

1. Data as a Base:

Mass personalization depends on collecting and analyzing relevant data about customers. This data can include purchasing history, preferences, online behavior, past interactions, and even demographic and business context information.

2. Advanced Segmentation:

B2B companies are using more advanced segmentation to group their customers into more specific categories. This allows them to offer customized solutions that address needs shared by a specific group of customers.
3. Automation Technology:
Technologies such as marketing automation and customer relationship management (CRM) systems allow companies to automate the personalization process, ensuring that the right messages and offers reach the right customers at the right time.
4. Customized Configuration:
Many B2B companies offer the ability to customize products or services to each customer's specific needs. This may involve choosing features, technical specifications, and other characteristics.
5. Smart Recommendations:
Companies are using recommendation algorithms to suggest products or solutions based on each customer's preferences and history. This helps to increase cross-sells and provide additional value.
6. Smart Self-Service:
Intelligent self-service platforms allow customers to explore and choose products, services or solutions based on their specific needs, without the need for direct human interaction.
7. Personalized Multichannel Interaction:
B2B companies are offering a consistent and personalized experience across different channels, whether through websites, social media, mobile apps or email communications.
Practical example:
A B2B software company implemented mass customization, offering software solutions tailored to each customer's specific needs. They collect information about each customer's operations and use this data to customize software settings and features, resulting in greater customer satisfaction and efficiency.
Mass customization in B2B commerce is becoming essential to meet customer expectations and stand out in a competitive market. By using data and technology intelligently, companies can create tailored experiences that add value to customers and establish lasting relationships.

8.4 New collaboration models between companies

Here are some emerging models of collaboration between companies in the B2B environment:
1. Partner Ecosystems:
Partner ecosystems involve creating networks of companies that collaborate to deliver comprehensive solutions to customers. Each company contributes its unique expertise to meet different aspects of a demand, expanding the value delivered.
2. Online Collaboration Platforms:
Online collaboration platforms allow companies to efficiently share information, knowledge and resources. This makes it easy to communicate, exchange ideas and collaborate on joint projects, regardless of geographic location.
3. Consortia and Strategic Alliances:
B2B companies are forming consortiums and strategic alliances to work together in specific areas. This could involve sharing resources, joint research and development, or even collaborative marketing.
4. Co-creation of Products/Services:
Companies collaborate from the early stages of creating products or services, combining their knowledge and resources to develop innovative solutions that meet market needs.
5. Marketplace Models and Trading Platforms:
B2B marketplaces are emerging as spaces where companies can connect to buy, sell and exchange products and services. These platforms promote collaboration between companies from different sectors.
6. Open Innovation:
Companies are opening their doors to external collaborations, seeking innovative solutions from startups, universities and other companies. This stimulates creativity and the exchange of knowledge.
7. R&D Collaboration:
Companies are forming partnerships to conduct joint research and development, sharing knowledge and resources to accelerate innovation.
8. Supplier and Distributor Networks:

Collaborations between suppliers, distributors and manufacturers allow for a more efficient supply chain, reducing costs and improving the quality of the final product.
9. Resource Sharing:
Companies are sharing physical resources, such as production facilities or equipment, to optimize utilization and reduce costs.
Practical example:
Several automotive manufacturers are collaborating on initiatives to develop electric cars, sharing knowledge about battery technologies and charging infrastructure. This allows them to more effectively address the challenges of electrification and promote the adoption of electric vehicles.
These collaboration models are enabling B2B companies to leverage their partners' strengths, achieve synergies, and create more innovative and comprehensive solutions. Collaboration between companies not only improves operational efficiency, but also drives value creation for everyone involved.

8.5 Preparing for the challenges and opportunities of the B2B future

As the B2B environment continues to evolve at a rapid pace, companies must be prepared to face the challenges and seize the opportunities that the future holds. Here are some essential guidelines for successfully navigating this changing landscape:
1. Agility and Flexibility:
Agility is a valuable asset for any company in the B2B environment. The ability to quickly adapt to new technologies, market trends and customer demands is critical to remaining competitive.
2. Continuous Learning:
The pursuit of continuous learning is a key factor for success in the B2B future. This includes staying up to date with the latest industry trends, technologies and practices to make informed decisions and innovate consistently.
3. Non-Customer Focus:
Maintaining focus on customer needs is crucial. Keeping up with changing customer expectations and adapting strategies

accordingly is critical to ensuring customer satisfaction and brand loyalty.

4. Innovation and Experimentation:

Companies must adopt a mindset of constant innovation. Experimenting with new approaches, technologies and business models can lead to surprising discoveries and competitive advantages.

5. Collaboration and Partnerships:

Collaborating with other companies, startups and even competitors can result in powerful synergies. Forming strategic partnerships can accelerate innovation and expand market opportunities.

6. Technology Adoption:

Technology will continue to play a central role in the B2B of the future. Companies must be willing to adopt new technologies such as AI, automation, advanced data analytics and the Internet of Things (IoT) to improve efficiency and decision-making.

7. Focus on Sustainability:

Sustainability will be a critical consideration in the B2B future. Companies should consider adopting sustainable practices in their operations, including the use of clean energy, waste reduction and responsible supply chain practices.

8. Adaptation Culture:

Creating an organizational culture that values adaptation and innovation is essential. Companies must encourage employees to embrace change and be willing to explore new approaches.

9. Attention to Cybersecurity:

With continued digitalization, cybersecurity becomes even more crucial. Companies must invest in robust protection of data and confidential information to prevent security breaches.

10. Trend Monitoring:

Being aware of emerging trends in the B2B market and relevant sectors is essential. This allows companies to anticipate changes and adjust their strategies accordingly.

By embracing these guidelines, companies will be well equipped to face the challenges and embrace the opportunities of the B2B future. Adaptability and the ability to constantly learn will be the keys to remaining relevant and successful in an ever-evolving landscape.